EduKate Me

*A Survival Guide for All New
School Employees: Unspoken
Rules for Working in a School*

ED YERGALONIS

ISBN: 978-1-4834-9344-2 (sc)
ISBN: 978-1-4834-9343-5 (e)

Library of Congress Control Number: 2018913339

Lulu Publishing Services rev. date: 11/19/2018

Contents

Preface
Why Do We Need This Book?

For almost four decades, when dealing with some personnel incident, I would sit in amazement and wonder to myself, "What would have possessed you to do this?" My usual follow-up to this question was, "Don't you have any common sense?" And when I would sit down and talk with the person as to why they did what they did, their first answer was, "No one ever told me." Did I have to tell you to breathe twelve times in a minute?

After hitting my head against the wall for years, yes, maybe I am slow learner, but I finally got it. For most people I had to basically tell them almost everything about working in a school, and yes, people I hired did not possess common sense.

For example, one time I had a paraprofessional who decided to engage in a fist fight with one of our students, off campus and on a weekend, and thought there was nothing wrong with this behavior. I was told, "Well, you know, it was not in school." I shook my head in bewilderment.

Another time, I had several support staff decide to create a little fundraising opportunity and decided to raffle off a basket full of XXX-rated videos and adult toys. They saw nothing wrong with displaying it on a counter in a high-traffic office for everyone to see. When I started to address this, I was told, "We did not sell any tickets to students." They thought it was acceptable. And this was done under a vice principal's nose. Incredible.

And finally, yes, I could probably go on forever. Should I have told a teacher not to enter into a romantic sexual affair with a student? I had to tell a teacher that—a well-educated person who had no common sense. Unbelievable.

As I evolved, in my hiring interview, I would spend time ensuring that I personally went over my *Ten Commandments for Working in a School,* along with several distinct caveats that I will cover in this book. As a matter of fact, in the latter stages of my career, I created a brief form that I would have the person sign with me, and I then placed this signed form in his or her personnel file. Then when an incident arose, we could revisit this together before I fired him or her.

What I learned over time made my life much easier and hopefully prolonged some careers. Please read and review this book because the career you save may be your own.

The Ten Commandments of Working in a School

1. Working in a school is all about relationships.

2. You must be an ambassador for your school.

3. You are part of the culture and climate of your school.

4. Know that politics are everywhere.

5. Get along with others; play nicely in the sandbox.

6. Your effort and attitude will determine your success.

7. Listen before you speak.

8. You are the adult—act like one.

9. Read everything you are given.

10. When in doubt, ask someone.

Notes:

Commandment Caveats

- Treat everyone with respect and dignity.
- Keep your hands off students.
- Watch what you say—use no sarcasm, racial or ethnic slurs, or sexual innuendo.
- Conduct only school business while you are in school.
- Be aware of the image that you portray on social media sites.
- Come to work daily, and come to work on time.
- Dress for success.
- All relationships with students must be professional in nature.
- Get along with people.

Notes:

Why Do You Want to Work in a School?

You got the job that you were looking for. You are now a school employee. It is important to pause for a moment to take a look at why you want to work in a school setting.

Let's think about some of the reasons you may have taken this job. Some reasons are obvious, and others may not be so clear. Try to understand what got you to where you are right now.

If you are a teacher, you just want to teach. It is that simple, and schools provide you that opportunity. If you are in a supporting role in the school, your reasons for choosing a school may be more varied:

- The hours are quite good and regular, with limited overtime.
- You may be entitled to an excellent benefits package.
- Depending on the position, you may have the summers off or have a reduced work schedule.
- In all likelihood, your travel to work is minimal.
- You want to be surrounded by children because you enjoy the energy and joy that they can bring to your life—the *best* reason.
- You want to be around your *own* children—maybe the *worst* reason.
- You may feel that you do not have to work very hard because there is a perception that it is easy to work in a school—a *foolish* reason.
- You needed a job, and that was the only one available.

For whatever reason, you have now joined the school community. And with that comes a responsibility. Within this community, there is an expectation that you will be the best person in that job.

Schools are unique places. They can chew you up and spit you out. Schools can be a source of joy for you, or they can bring you an enormous amount of emotional pain. It is up to you. This book will help you navigate your journey. These unspoken rules that I will share with you may actually determine your success or failure in this job. If you are a new teacher, this book is not about pedagogy. This book is about survival. Remember this first rule that I will share.

Notes:

It Is All about Relationships

You have chosen a people business. Everything you do will involve working with people. In addition to being part of the overall team of the school, during your career you will be required to be part of many different smaller teams and groups. Collaboration is a must. Working in a school is not for the lone wolf, no matter what position you hold.

Your first piece of required reading is Robert Fulghum's work *All I Needed to Know I Learned in Kindergarten: Uncommon Thoughts on Common Things* (1989). This small book says it all. If we could all just follow his words of wisdom in this book, our work environment would be a better place. I would also bet that perhaps instead of dreading to come to work, we all would really enjoy the experience. We all have learned what Fulghum shares. But why do we forget what he shares so easily? Perhaps the better question is why we situationally forget his words of wisdom. Listed below are the major points from this work:

- Share.
- Play fair.
- Don't hit people.
- Put things back.
- Clean up your own mess.
- Say you are sorry when you hurt someone.
- Wash your hands before you eat.
- Flush.
- Warm cookies and cold milk are good for you.
- Live a balanced life.
- Take a nap every day.
- When you go out into the world, watch out for traffic, hold hands, and stick together.

- Be aware of wonder.
- Everything dies—so do we.

If we were to live by these simple rules in the workplace, there would be no need for this book. Likewise, many years ago when I first starting coaching, I brought my team together on the first day of practice and explained my team rules. I only had one. And that rule was to just *do the right thing*. Perhaps I was a bit naive. Little did I know that many of my players did not know what the right thing was. Many of my players—just like many of the staff that I have hired—lacked common sense. I had a horrific year. The next year I came back with an elaborate set of team rules in booklet form. I tried to leave nothing for chance. You see, I learned a valuable lesson during that first year. Namely, I had to tell everyone what the right thing was. I had to tell them what to do and what to say. I had to teach them how to be part of our team. We had a much better year.

Perhaps I am just thickheaded because when I became a principal, once again I operated with simplicity, thinking that my adult staff would know how to do the right thing. Once again, I was proven wrong. I had to regroup for the next year and commit everything to writing. I tried to leave no stone unturned. I tried to make these expectations come alive. I was now on the road to success. Let's now get on the road to success together and review these commonsense rules that apply to all schools. No matter what role you have in the school, whether it is the principal or the newly hired paraprofessional, I encourage you to follow these rules. Additionally, you must model these rules for others, especially if you are in a leadership position. This book is intended to be a simple, quick read. A book that is easy to remember. A book that is easy to follow. A book that is easy to internalize. A book that just makes sense.

Notes:

You Must Be an Ambassador for Your School

Now that you have been hired, it is essential that you become a true ambassador for your school. That may sound a bit strange, but in today's competitive world, if you want to survive, you have to be able to market and sell your product. And in this case, the product is your school and the education that you are providing to the children. In some cases, depending on what type of school in which you are working, your job may be dependent upon your enrollment. If your enrollment goes, so goes your job. Always seek to increase your enrollment. Do not take it for granted.

I have seen some people become cavalier in their attitude about this notion. They just don't get it. These employees forget that the children and the families that they serve are their clients. Ask any salesperson—if your clients are not happy, then they will take their business elsewhere. This has become a reality. It has become the survival of the fittest. I strongly believe that if the playing surface is level, competition is great for everyone. Competition will make you better—but it will make you better only if you care and choose to compete.

Being an ambassador for your school goes far beyond not saying anything bad about your programs. Being an ambassador requires that you are constantly talking positively about your school. You must accentuate the positive. No matter how cloudy the day seems, you must always see the sunshine. You must be "the glass is half-full" type of person. Let's face it—every school has its share of warts. You do not have to advertise them!

Many discussions and decisions about your school are made on the Saturday morning local soccer field, at the grocery store, at the local coffee shop, or even at the local adult watering hole. It is at these venues that the community will gather to discuss the pros and cons of your school—and perhaps the pros and cons of you personally. And most times the positives are not discussed. The negatives receive all of the greatest passion and focus. These stories do not have to be accurate, and most times they are not. They may hold a smidgen of truth, but the remainder is the result of the old telephone game. If you and your family live and play in your school community, you must be aware of this and use these opportunities to sell the school. You will quickly find that when you do your grocery shopping or are wandering in a mall, you will be greeted by your students. I can vividly recall one time when one of my middle school students was amazed that I food shopped. Students have a unique perspective on the adults in their building. Be careful, inasmuch as some of your friends are apt to pump you for inside information. Also, remember that when you are out with a group of friends and have a couple of glasses of wine, your lips become loose. Watch it. This is not your venue to vent your frustrations. Be cautious! Please use your common sense even if you are in a hurry. Most times when you prepare yourself in a hurry, it looks like it. Make the first impression a lasting one. You will never get a second chance.

Notes:

Look Like a Champion

Before you leave for work, ask yourself the following questions:

- *Does my attire meet the expectations or code of my school?*
- *Is my hair combed? Is my beard well-trimmed?*
- *Are my clothes cleaned and pressed?*
- *Am I clean? What about my hands and fingernails?*
- *Are my shoes appropriate for my job?* For example, those rubber or plastic beach or shower shoes have no place in the work environment. Not only are they a safety concern, but they also look cheap. They are great for your vacation, but not for your school.
- *Should I wear a tie?* I know that for men, wearing a tie has lost some of the appeal it once had. Maybe I am old-fashioned, but the tie communicates that something important is going on here. If someone important was coming to visit you, in all likelihood you would put a tie on. Aren't your students important? Over the course of my career, I have flip-flopped on this notion. I am back attitudinally in support of the tie. Try it. I guarantee your students will respond differently to you when you are wearing that tie.
- *Did I look in the mirror before I left the house?* Believe it or not, I think some people do not own a mirror. And if they did, it must be hidden in such a place that they forget to look at it. I get it. When I look at myself, I wish I was thinner and had more hair, but I still force myself to look. You have to look beyond your personal flaws or pet peeves and see what other people see. Do you want others to see what you are seeing in the mirror? Do you even care? *You should!*

- *What type of pants am I wearing?* This may be a bit of an odd question, but for me it is an important one. What is the obsession with denim blue jeans? My mother would have called them dungarees. They were my play clothes. When **I** see teachers wearing blue jeans, I cringe. Maybe this is my personal hang-up, but to me it sends a clear message. The message when you are wearing blue jeans is, "I was doing some yard work and decided to come in and teach." This is not the message that I want my staff conveying to the students or the parents they encounter. Of course, I know that some of these pants can cost hundreds of dollars and you may look very nice in them and they are comfortable. But too many of these jeans, are old, crusty, and faded. I abhor the jeans that are thin by nature and now have been worn through. I worry that when you may bend over, your rear end will be hanging out. It also amazes me the amount of time and energy spent by some to circumvent this issue. I know of a principal who wanted to or was convinced by staff to have a dress down day every Friday. No way. This was merely a circumvention of my rule. Likewise, the fundraiser to wear the jeans has to go. People will pay a great deal of money to have this privilege. Why not just donate to your favorite charity? Another way around this rule is to have a school spirit day. I have found that teachers will do anything to wear jeans. (I did finally allow it for a spirit day once a month. Although I think this had little to do with school spirit and more to do with wearing the jeans.) While we are on the subject of pants, think long and hard about the appropriateness of those skin-tight legging type of pants. Some people just do not have the figure to pull this style off. I know I wouldn't be able to wear them. No one needs to see your underwear or every contour of your body. Go back and review my statement about mirrors. *Take a look at yourself and be honest!*
- *Are my undergarments exposed?* Wear your sundress to the beach or to the nightclub. They are not meant for school. Of course, I know that times change and these changes will dictate what is considered appropriate. Years ago, a woman would never leave the house if a bra strap was exposed. Today it is almost a style. However, I still do not believe that the students need to see your

undergarments. Let's extend this example to middle school and high school boys. And yes, perhaps this is a bit sexist, but I have seen young men in this age group get the wrong impression from their teachers when they dress this way. Yes, it is wrong, and this would be a great lesson to teach and instill maturity in these guys, but I do not think the trade-off is worth it. Use your head.

- *Can I show off my six pack?* It is nice to be fit and in shape, and I am sure that you are quite proud of it. But your students do not need to see this. Nor do they need to see that nice, stylish belly button ring. Save these clothes for the weekend and the beach.
- *What message are my tattoos sending?* I am not at all against tattoos, yet I would think twice about where I place them on my body. I have thought about getting a tattoo many times, but if I did, knowing the field that I have chosen for my career, I would think long and hard about where I would place it on my body.

I feel now somewhat assured that you look good when you leave your house in the morning. Now let's take a look at how you greet people.

Notes:

Communicate Like a Champion

If we all could follow this rule, perhaps there would be no need for other rules. Our discussion would be over. But let us not kid ourselves; we need a deeper discussion of this topic. You must be a master communicator. Very often, any problem at work can be traced back to a failure in communication. Think about the following points:

- Watch your language. Never use profanity and never tell a joke that would be considered dirty or filled with sexual innuendo.
- Treat everyone with respect and dignity. Remember the Golden Rule!
- Never make any discriminatory remarks. Always be sensitive to race, gender, religion, and orientation.
- Speak for yourself, and do not volunteer for others.
- Do not mumble.
- Say it, don't spray it. Be cognizant of your saliva. No one needs a bath from your conversation.
- Respect everyone's confidentiality.
- Let someone finish their sentence and thought. No interruptions please!
- Respect others' workspace.
- Listen to what others say.
- Never gossip or talk about others, and do not repeat stories. Never engage in the telephone game.
- When you are not sure of something, seek clarification.
- If you made an error, apologize and attempt to fix it.
- There are several taboo topics. Never talk about personal health issues, politics, relationships, and your sex life. Keep your thoughts on these topics to yourself.

- Know what messages your body language sends.
- Do not force your beliefs or values on others.
- Avoid stereotypes.
- Speak or write clearly. Pretend that you are the listener or reader of what you want to say.
- Do not engage in power struggles. You will not win. There will be no winners.
- Be positive, not negative in your outlook. See the glass as half full, not half empty. No one wants to be around a constantly negative person.
- Say what needs to be said and move along.

Notes:

Know Your Body Language

It is true that you never get a second chance to make a good first impression. Your appearance helps you maintain credibility and respect. It is also important to be aware of the nonverbal messages you are sending out. Personally, sometimes I have a hard time with this. However, I aware of this and always work on it. Some cues are:

- Look at the person.
- Sit or stand up straight.
- Smile.
- Don't roll your eyes.
- Do not sigh in disgust or disagreement.
- Don't use body language to show disappointment or dejection.
- Don't chew gum.
- Carry yourself with confidence. Walk like a winner, a champion. You do not have to be a big person to have a big presence. It is all in the way you enter a room and carry yourself. On the other hand, you do not have to be the school bully.

I have visited many schools, and it seems that most school secretaries cannot be bothered with greeting me. I apologize if I am painting with too broad of a brush here, but nonetheless, it is an impression I am continually left with. This is usually my first impression. To them, my visit is a distraction. When someone greets me in a professional and appropriate manner, I make it a point to tell them, and if I am meeting with their boss, I make sure I tell him or her. This goes a long way. Sometimes they will even share with me that I am a big disruption to their day. And let us not forget the body language that can be emitted from behind a desk. If looks could kill, I would be already dead. That is disappointing. When the first ambassador of the school that I encounter sends out such a negative impression, I know that not only would I not want to work there, but I definitely would not want to send my children there. Smile a little. Be helpful. Show that it is a pleasure meeting and serving people. Even on a bad day, work to pull that off. Remember that you are happy to be there! Show it!

Notes:

Use the Telephone Correctly

I know this may sound a little odd, but try to employ the same strategies you use when you personally meet someone when you meet them on the telephone. Let's remember our rule about first impressions. Let us also remember our personal frustration when you are trying to solve a credit card problem with a customer service representative four thousand miles away from you. It is frustrating and disappointing and can paint a very bad image of your product. And in your case at work, it is your school. Please do not think you will never answer a phone at work. Although it may not be your job, you will be called upon to perform this service. So the next time that you answer a phone, think about the following:

- Speak clearly and loud enough to be heard.
- Identify yourself and your location.
- Answer the call promptly with a pleasant tone in your voice. If your school has a special motto or manner in which to answer the phone, use it. I recall at one school that had an initiative to improve character education, someone would always answer the phone like this: "Good morning, this is Jane Doe at Madison School, where character counts. How can I help you?" What a pleasant way to be greeted. Try it.
- This is not a time for small talk
- Pay attention. Serve the person on the other end.
- If you need to transfer the call, do so, yet provide the caller with the correct extension.
- If you are taking a message, make sure you get it correct, with a proper name and a callback number.

- Promptly deliver the message to the intended person.
- Do not end the call with anger, yet do not subject yourself to abuse. If the caller is abusive, politely tell him or her that you cannot continue the conversation in this manner. If this continues, end the call and have a supervisor promptly return the call. Most importantly, be civil!

Always remember that the telephone is an essential tool needed to conduct business. Use it correctly.

Notes:

Know the Message
Your Coffee Sends

Is it necessary for you to walk around the building with your cup of coffee? I know for me, this was always a big turnoff. In one breath we will tell students that they are not allowed to eat and drink throughout the building, and yet the adults walk around drinking their coffee.

Additionally, if you are called into a parent meeting, and coffee is not provided for all, I would not expect you to be sitting there drinking your coffee. It does not send a good message. I have seen adults enter a parental meeting drinking coffee and eating a donut and then slouch in a chair with crumbs all over the place and expect to conduct an important meeting.

While we are talking about coffee, I was never happy if a staff member walked into my meeting late coming from outside of the building drinking their Dunkin Donuts or Starbucks coffee. The meeting has started, and you parade in with your coffee. I know, you estimated your time wrong, got caught in unexpected traffic, or had a situation that developed as you were leaving. I really do not care about your excuse. If I am the boss in your school, I am not happy.

Notes:

Be Neat and Clear, Check Your Spelling, and Check Your Grammar

I have terrible handwriting. I heard a secretary behind my back tell another secretary that she was tired of reading my "childlike scrawl." I let her know that I heard her. She was embarrassed, and we were able to joke about this. However, she was right! I would never turn in a handwritten paper to a professor or use my handwriting in a professional arena. Think about the message one sends when a note goes home to a parent that is nothing more than scribbles on a piece of paper. I always wanted to ask people why they just did not use the crayons to communicate. At least it would have been colorful. Even if you use your computer to generate a note, is everything spelled correctly? Is your grammar correct? Are your tests professionally prepared? Spelled correctly? Neat? Remember that you are an ambassador! What message are you sending to parents if you send home information chock full of misspellings or grammatical errors?

I know if I was that parent, I would question the person's credibility and that of the principal or director. Everything reflects back up to the boss. And yes, you want to keep the boss happy.

Notes:

Be a Problem Solver

Whatever your role may be, do it to the best of your ability. If you are a teacher, be the best teacher in your district. If you are a custodian, make sure your area is the cleanest in the school. Likewise, if you are a secretary, be the best and most efficient secretary there is. You get my point here. Be the best employee you can be. Your job status means nothing. Many times, I would hear a person say, "But I am only a custodian" or "I am only a cafeteria aide." I really do not care. Be the best custodian or paraprofessional you can be.

Show initiative, and be a problem-solver! Go the extra mile. If you have to deliver bad news to the boss, come with several suggestions to improve the situation. If I have to do your job for you, then perhaps I do not need you. Think about that.

Notes:

You Have a Responsibility in the Development of the School Culture and Climate

Wow! You may think that this is a pretty complex rule. I assure you, it is not. First, let us take a moment to provide some working definitions of climate and culture. It is really pretty simple. Steve Gruenert and Todd Whitaker in their book *School Culture Rewired* (2015) present one of the clearest and easiest to understand messages on culture. They describe the culture as the school's *personality*, based on values and beliefs that take years to evolve. School climate is best defined as the group's *attitude* that can be very changeable. Climate is what you do, and culture is why you do it (Gruenert and Whitaker). Everyone in the school community is responsible for culture and climate. *It is not solely the principal's job!* When everyone is working together, the school will be a very pleasant place to work. The school will have the potential of accomplishing many great things. When something is afoul in these areas, you may hate coming to work. And if you hate coming to work, how will it be for the students? At times I thought wouldn't it be wonderful to place all of the malcontents in one school? I wanted to place all of these miserable people on an island. I could fill each role. There are miserable principals, teachers, paraprofessionals, custodians, and secretaries. You name the position and I can find a miserable person to fill it. However, there is one problem with this thought. What child would you send there? Always understand that one person can ruin the culture and climate of your school. Will this be you?

Know the Strategic Plan and Mission of the School and District

Is it critical that you know about the strategic plan and mission of your school? Some may argue that it is not. However, I disagree. Much can be learned about a school and a district from the mission statement. I do not believe it is necessary to memorize these standards, but it is important that you understand them to more fully know how you and your job assignment fit in. More importantly, does the mission statement come alive? Can you see it in the schools? I am not talking about seeing a sign on the wall. I am talking about can you see it in the way people work together, interact with the children, maintain the building, etc. You should be able to see it in almost everything in the school.

These statements are usually long philosophical statements that identify some lofty goals. Each person contributes in their own way. Do not forget this. Of course, everyone is entitled to a bad day. But when these bad days become the norm, there is a problem. Think about this, and honestly pause to reflect to see if you and your attitude are the root of this problem.

Notes:

It Is All about Effort and Attitude

It cannot get any simpler. If you come to work every day and try hard with a positive attitude, I almost can guarantee that you will be a success. I will also guarantee that your colleagues will enjoy working with you, and likewise the students will find that they want to be around you. That being said, this effort and attitude concept is my golden rule. And if everyone followed this, we would never need another manual or rulebook. However, you and I both know that not everyone can follow this. It is amazing to me the way some people spend a great deal of time figuring out how to get out of their work. They should only put that type of energy and commitment into their work. I would never get upset and be very forgiving to someone who tried hard and had a great attitude.

There is a wonderful philosophy developed by a group of workers at Pike's Fish Market in Seattle, Washington. This group of men figured out how to make a mundane job exciting on a daily basis. There has been a great deal of publicity around this place, and they have marketed their concept quite well. I would bet that you have already seen some of their work. The Fish Philosophy has four components:

- **Choose Your Attitude**: Each day when you get out of bed you can choose what attitude you will have. Will you be bright, energetic, and happy? Or will you be a sourpuss? It is your choice!
- **Be There**: When you are interreacting with a person, make sure you stay in the moment and focus on them. Focus on what you are talking about in the specific instant. Don't let your mind wonder about everything but what you are talking about. Focus!

- **Make Their Day:** Work to make your client or customer's day a better day. Never forget that the children are your clients. Without them, you have no job!
- **Have Fun**: There is certainly nothing wrong with having fun at work. Of course, this fun must be appropriate to the setting. When you have some fun at work, you will have a better day. I am sure of that (Charthouse).

It is so simple. Give it a try.

Notes:

Understand and Live by the Norms of Your School

A norm can be simply and commonly defined as what is the standard procedure. A norm is the typical and usual way things are done in a group by the individuals in that group. For our purposes, let us consider the group as your school. People usually religiously follow school norms. I would bet if you asked a veteran staff member why people do a certain thing, they would probably answer because it was always done that way. Now that is a norm. Hold tight. Not all norms are good.

It is important that you follow the unwritten norms and rules for your school. You want to fit in. Let's start out by talking about *coming to work on time.* You will and should get fired quickly if you cannot abide by this. Let's dig a bit deeper. What about coming back from break or lunch on time? Some people think that this is unimportant. If you think this way you are *wrong.* Breaks and lunch are usually tied together. If you do not leave or return on time, you are throwing everything off. The next person, in all likelihood, will not be able to take their break or lunch until you return. Each person depends on the other person. Likewise, when you are given an hour for lunch, it means an hour. Those five extra minutes will turn into ten, and before you know it, you are taking an hour and a half lunch. Your boss will never know. He or she is too busy to check up on you. But that should not be the reason that you return on time. You return on time because that is the right thing to do. Be consistent and considerate because it is the right thing to do.

What about attendance in general? In most schools you will be given a bank of sick days. This is another advantage of working in a school. These days are to be used when you are sick! They are not free days for you to use during the year merely because you have them. I can recall a colleague, upon retiring from the district after thirty-five years, had zero days saved or accumulated. And he never had a long-term illness. He was blessed with good health. He was of the belief that these days were his to use regardless of his health. Stay home when you are sick. Nobody wants to catch your cold or flu. But push yourself when you are tired. I am not an advocate of mental health days. Schools have a very difficult time finding substitutes. In some of your positions a sub will never be sought. When this happens, your colleagues are impacted by your absence because they will be called upon to do more during their day. They will have to also do your job. This will erode a school's morale quicker than anything else. A perfect example of this is when a custodian is out. For years, I did not have a substitute pool for custodians, and so whenever one person was out, the others would have to divide his work and complete it during their regular shift. And when this occurred, classrooms were not as clean as they should have been. The custodians were angry, and now the teachers were angry. Soon the students would be angry, and of course the boss was now angry. Tomorrow the parents would call to express their anger—all because a custodian was absent. If the custodian was not sick, he or she should be at work. Your absence caused a ripple effect. Be concerned.

Notes:

Wear Your Identification Badge

It is essential that your identification badge be displayed at all times. This is a standard safety procedure. It is critical that only authorized people be in the building at any given time. Some staff will take a "who cares" attitude about this topic. They will have a ton of excuses, such as:

- Everyone knows me.
- I left it in the car.
- My picture stinks.
- It is in my desk, briefcase, closet, bookbag, etc.
- I forgot it at home.

Why are educators so reluctant to comply with this rule? If you were to visit a place of business, you would be required to wear a visitor's ID. Likewise, take a look at the employees from the CEO on down, and you will see that they all have their badge in place.

This is especially true in these unpredictable times of violence in schools. People need to know who is supposed to be there. There should be not tolerance for noncompliance in this regard. We must take every measure to help make our schools safe.

I used to find it quite humorous when staff would lament and blame me for our students not wearing their badges. I finally realized that if it is not important to the adults, how can we get the students to comply? I remain convinced that we could have solved this problem in less than a week if everyone thought it was important. I stopped letting my staff scapegoat me on this. It never became a norm. It never became part of the culture of the building.

Know Your Facility

Make it an important task for you to walk your building and grounds and learn where the key places are. Even though in your role you may never visit some of these places, it is essential that you know their location. You need to be an informed and knowledgeable employee about your place of work.

Notes:

Know Your Community

If you are lucky, your school onboarding procedures will include a tour of the community. If not, I strongly recommend that you take a driving or walking tour of your town. It is important to find out where the students are coming from. When you know this, you may be a little more compassionate when you are about to mark a student tardy on that cold, snowy day when you know where your students are walking from. It is also important to know specific landmarks in the town because they will serve as a reference point for you and the students. For example, identify where the town's library, city hall, police station, recreation center, YMCA, shopping centers (where your students may work), significant industry, or other noteworthy landmarks are. Having knowledge of this information will make it easier for you to build those important relationships with your students.

Notes:

Run Away from Rumors and Gossip

The quickest path to the destruction of the culture and the climate of your building is to feed off gossip and rumors. It is a destructive practice. You will be told what you need to know when you need to know it. Do not let your work station become the bitching post for the school or district. I have seen secretaries hold court with all the malcontents during the day at their desk. It becomes a constant stream of complainers and miserable people. The same goes for a reception area or security post. I had safety officers, as they walked the building, who would be the messengers of the school's rumors and dirt. Can you imagine that? They were traveling malcontents who just loved to make other people miserable. For example, they started a rumor about layoffs and watched people scramble. I have seen people get physically sick all because of a rumor. Likewise, my librarian at one time would love to start the rumor. He would add a piece of credible information to a crazy story, and the next thing you know, it was around the building like a wildfire. When it got to me, I knew exactly who started it. I would confront him, and he would be disappointed that it took so long. Was he a sadist? I don't know, but he thought it was hilarious. People will make a point to stop at specific locations frequently during the day to catch up on the rumor of the minute. This is an unhealthy practice. Stay away from it.

Each school will also have an informal yet designated (never official) complaint room. This is most likely the faculty room or the faculty dining area. I encourage new teachers to stay out of these places. Perhaps find a different place to eat your lunch. Maybe a group of teachers with similar positive attitudes could gather together in a classroom to share a meal. In most schools, the faculty room is the area of complaining and gossiping.

I used to find it a bit comical when I was the principal. I would wander into the faculty room. All conversation would cease. I would make some small talk, but I knew they wanted me to get the heck out of there. You can survive nicely without going there. Be strong. Complainers and malcontents love company!

Notes:

Understand That Politics Are Everywhere

Schools are remarkable political places. You might not be reading this book if it was not for politics. You may have gotten your job because of who you know and not what you know. I am sure somewhere along the way there was a personal connection of some sort. I know for me, when I was looking at a stack of a hundred resumes for a teaching job, I would get a call from a board member asking me to take a look at a specific candidate. I would comply, telling the board member that I would interview this candidate, but I reminded that person I was still hiring the best candidate for the job. Unfortunately, depending upon the specific situation and depending upon the vacancy and of course depending on the pressure applied, sometimes the candidate chosen was not the best. Luckily, recent nepotism laws have helped curb this. But believe me, it still exists. And it may seem that if you do not play these political games, you will not survive.

It is important that you understand this. You will encounter internal school politics as soon as you enter your school. Some may have met these politics when they arrived to the parking lot because in many places parking lot rules are established politically. You must identify the power brokers in your school. And most times, these individuals are not the administration. And more importantly, you must learn how to work with these power brokers.

Two of the most important people you will meet in your school are the head secretary, which is most likely the principal's secretary, and the head custodian. These two individuals will go a long way in the determining the success of your stay at your school. They should be spoken to with respect and reverence because if you do not, they can make your life miserable.

Both of these individuals control information, access, and services. Without cooperation, you will not survive.

Notes:

Know and Respect the Chain of Command

It is important that you know the chain of command and live within its framework. There could be times that an innocent comment could be taken the wrong way by someone and ultimately cause you trouble. I spoke earlier in this chapter about how a person may have obtained his or her job. He or she knew someone. I get it. It is all part of the politics and games that work in a school. But you can't run back to this person every time something happens that you may not like. And never forget my rule that states that you must remain an ambassador for your school. When your friend, the board member, asks you how your job is going, I trust that you will paint a positive picture of your experience to date. Badmouthing the school or your boss is not the way to go. Likewise, this same board member may ask you if you need anything. If this is asked, please respond that your boss is taking care of everything. I can recall one time early in my coaching career, I was asked by a board member if I needed anything for my program. I was naïve at the time and proceeded to tell him my laundry list of desires. He in turn went back and began to rip the superintendent for not being attentive to my needs. It was not long thereafter that I was called into the superintendent's office and was given a good chewing out for going behind his back and over his head. That was never my intention. I was asked a question and answered it honestly. I was young and foolish and trusting. I learned a good lesson! Be careful what you say and to whom you say it.

Know Your Evaluators

Always know who is responsible for your evaluation and who may contribute to this process. Never hesitate to check in with them to find out how you are doing, but do not be a pain in this regard. It is also critical that if an administrator asks you to do something, you do it. If it was not in the scope of your job, you can seek a remedy after the fact. If the administrator who asked you to perform some task is not your direct boss, complete what was asked anyway. Even though he or she may not be in the sphere of influence, he or she is still an administrator. Do not be insubordinate.

For whatever reason, if you are uncomfortable with this request, ask to talk privately to this person and share your concerns. If you still have the same comfort level, move up the chain of command and document your efforts. By the same token, do not comply with a request that you feel is illegal or unethical. If you deem this is the case, state that to the person asking you to do whatever task it may be. Immediately move to the next person in the chain of command and state your concerns.

Notes:

Listen and Be Receptive to Feedback

Be careful what you wish for! Many people have asked me what I thought about something, and it seemed like an eternity before I answered. I took this long preparing my answer because I was not looking to hurt this person. And I knew if I told the truth and was honest, this person was not really ready for the truth. So, I played the usual game and ducked the candid conversation. However, if we are mature adults, we must always be ready for candid feedback. What you do with the feedback is entirely up to you. Listed below are some simple guidelines. It is an important topic.

- Listen and do not interrupt or respond immediately.
- Listen to what is being said, not to how it is being said.
- Ask questions about what is being said.
- Control your body language. Do not withdraw, and do not pout.
- Do not become combative.
- Take this opportunity to refocus your goals or reestablish your priorities.
- Once you receive feedback, keep it to yourself.
- As you receive this feedback, although this may be difficult, try not to take it personally.
- Do not feel compelled to fill dead time with conversation.
- Always ask the person for specifics and evidence of the action being discussed (McCarthy).
- Finally, it is important to thank the person for giving you the feedback. Feedback will allow you an opportunity to grow. Look at it this way: the person did you a service (Hindy).

Understand How to Use Your Technology

Technology helps you get your job done. It helps us problem solve. It helps us mine data to inform decision making. You must know how to use all available technology, and if you do not, ask someone and it may behoove you to take a professional development course based upon your needs. Remember the following:

- Your school email remains the property of the school, and all messages are archived.
- Do not use this email for personal use.
- Do not expect privacy in this regard.
- Do not reply to all in a broadcast group email.
- Do not reply to an email with a particular subject when you are talking about an entirely different subject.
- Do not complain about an issue being fixed when you have never submitted an order to your help desk.
- It is perfectly acceptable, if applicable, to have students teach and help you with technology. In all likelihood, they know more than you.
- Use *help* menus.
- Do not be afraid of YouTube for help.
- Do not use or play with your technology at a meeting.
- Just because you can Google a subject very quickly, that does not make you an expert on the topic, nor does it make what you found a fact. Not everything you read on the Internet is true!
- Each district and school will have some form of an acceptable use policy. It is critical that you know and understand what can and what cannot be done on your school's computers.

- You are not to add any hardware or software to the school system without the express consent of the district.
- If you have access to the student database, you are only to use it as it applies to your job. For example, it is not ethical for you to go look at your neighbor's child's grades to compare them to your own child.
- Do not waste time or clog up the system with humor or senseless "forward this message" type of emails.
- When using your email, know your audience and what language is acceptable for use. Can you use abbreviations? Does grammar count? Does spelling count? These concepts become part of the norms of the school. However, if I am e-mailing the boss, I would make sure all my i's are dotted and my t's crossed.
- Use an electronic signature whenever possible with your title and phone number.

Use good judgment and common sense.

Notes:

Abide by Appropriate Social Media Guidelines

Be wise with all of your social media outlets. Yes, I know that it has been tested in the courts, and I believe you have every right to put what you want on your social media sites. But think about it. Do you want your parents or community members to come across your Facebook page or some other current source and see a picture of you doing something that you may not be proud of? And personally, I never want to hear when there is a problem that you thought this page was private. Things have a funny way of becoming public. I have had numerous parents throw Facebook pages across my desk when complaining about a staff member. I became embarrassed for that staff person. If information is on the Internet about you, you can just about rest assured that a community member will see it. When this happens, will you be proud of what they find? You are now the adult, and your college fraternity and sorority days are over. Make sure your sites reflect you, the person, in a positive way. And please do not argue that your site is private. Once again, use good common sense. Wow, there are those two words again—*common sense*. How many times have you read that already?

Notes:

Understand and Respect Confidentiality

By the nature of your job, at times you will both see and hear confidential items. What is said in school, stays in school. What is seen in school stays in school. You may be privy to a situation that happens with your neighbor's child who lives right down the street. This could be a friend of yours. Or it could be someone you dislike. Regardless of your feelings about this situation, the family business is not to be repeated. Be careful with the soccer moms and dads on Saturday morning on your local athletic field. Just like the faculty rooms, these places are notorious spots for gossiping. I have seen people so engrossed in the local gossip they do not even see or care about their own child on the field. *You cannot enter into these conversations!*

Notes:

Keep Outside Business Interests Outside of the School

When you are working in the school, you are working in the school. Keep all other business interests out of this environment. For example, if you are the principal's secretary, do not set up your daughter's girl scout cookie sales display on the main office counter. Unacceptable.

You may be a tax preparation expert. You cannot post on your workspace your tax office hours. Unacceptable.

You son's soccer league is doing a fundraising tricky tray. You become the spot in the building for purchasing raffle chances. You also avail yourself the opportunity to strongarm people as they walk into the office. Unacceptable.

You are there to do your job. Only your job. Do it.

Notes:

Be Legal, Ethical, and Right

You may be placed in a predicament at times when you are in doubt as to what is the right thing to do. My best advice here is to merely ask someone who has some experience and someone you trust. Ask your boss. Ask a union delegate. Ignorance is no excuse for breaking a rule or doing something that is unethical.

I also strongly encourage you to read all policy and procedure manuals in addition to handbooks that are issued to you. I know that once issued, these books tend to remain unopened and probably dumped into a dark closet or drawer someplace. If you are a union employee, read and understand your contract. Once these items are issued, you become responsible for the contents of same. It is essential that you have a working knowledge of these items.

When you are faced with a situation that causes you to be in a quandary, I ask you to reflect upon certain items. The first one that always comes to mind is something a former mentor of mine once told me. He asked me to always think about how the situation I was handling would look written up in tomorrow's paper. When I did this, the answer usually provided guidance to me. The next thing I would think about—and this became clearer to me as my own children became adults—is what advice would I give them in the same situation. I would then follow my own advice. Always make sure that what you are thinking about doing is legal and in line with all school and district policies and procedures. Once again, if you do, it is hard to be wrong. And finally, if you ever start to have thoughts about how no one will ever find out the truth or that you can destroy all evidence of it, it is time to rethink your actions. Always remember that someone will eventually find out, and your actions could become inexplicable. Also, remember that the cover-up is always worse than the crime. If you think that you can get away with what you are thinking just this once, you are headed for trouble. Perhaps you rationalize by saying that everyone does it. No, everyone does not do it. I have heard people tell me that they thought no one would ever find out. Wrong again.

I would also think long and hard if a colleague was to say to me, "Hey, we didn't have this conversation. You didn't hear this from me." Get far away. Get very far away. Trouble is coming.

Notes:

Complete All Forms and Paperwork on Time

All paperwork needs to be submitted completed and on time. End of the story. Of course, all paperwork must be completed honestly! People are dependent upon you submitting things according to schedule. Although you may not be aware of the specific reason around each, just understand that there is a reason. No one is asking you to do something just to personally torture you.

Notes:

Get Along with People. Play Nicely in the Sandbox!

Take a moment to think about all the people you interact with in a given day. And yes, you have to get along with all of these people. Life in a school is like a big sandbox, and we have to play together nicely. Some general guidelines include:

- Establish a respectful environment with respectful interactions and cooperation. Speak kindly to one another.
- The workplace must be free of all forms of harassment, discrimination, and bullying. These behaviors cannot be tolerated in a work environment.
- Strive to be a lifelong learner.
- You must be honest and trustworthy.
- Be empathic and compassionate to your coworkers and students.
- Your deeds say more than your words. Learn to live by this credo.
- Enjoy and celebrate the success of your colleagues. There is no room for pettiness and jealousy.
- Go the extra mile, and be a problem solver.
- Show pride in your work.
- Always be prepared.
- Follow the norms and rules of your workplace.
- Practice self-discipline.
- Be a stand-up person. Take responsibility for your actions, and honor your commitment.
- Be fair and consistent in your dealings with others.

Do Not Annoy Others

Let's face it. We can all annoy others at times. It might be hard to believe, yet it is true. Believe it or not, we all will do things that annoy others. I am sure that your parents or a significant other will affirm that assertion. Some people can annoy more than others. Probably by this time in their life, it is too hard or too late to change, but we must be cognizant of this. And in all likelihood, you are not going to be able to change that person. To effectively change, that person must want to change. Take some time to think about the following annoying behaviors that many are guilty of:

- Loud, obnoxious, or impolite behaviors
- Being consistently late
- Leaving machines in a state of disrepair or out of supplies, like the copy machine and the laminator
- Extremely nosy, always looking to get into your business, looking at your desk, looking at your computer screen
- Every conversation is dominated by this person. You cannot get a word in. A conversation becomes a monologue.
- Accepts no personal responsibility for anything. Blames everyone but themselves.
- Me-me-me-me. It is always about them.
- Body odor, bad breath, unclean clothes, or too much perfume. Do you stink? Do you brush your teeth? Do you dump that entire bottle of cologne or perfume on yourself every morning? Some people I could smell coming before I saw them. Think about this.

Avoid Conflict and Controversy

You are surrounded by a lot of people. You are going to like some people and not others. Likewise, some people are not going to like you. We live and work in a big world. Think about the following items when you sense a conflict is upon you:

- Think before you speak—always. There is no need to hurry to respond. Do not let your head get ahead of your brain.
- If you sense a problem coming in your area, get away from it. Go for a walk, go to the bathroom—just get away. Gather your emotions, and do not respond when you are emotional.
- Always be a good listener, and seek clarification. Do not jump the gun on your response.
- Know everyone's personal boundaries and space.
- Praise rather than criticize.
- Do not overreact to a situation.
- *Watch your body language and tone. Sometimes it is not what you said but how you said it that makes people upset.*
- Remember, this is work, not a party.
- Always keep your hands off of another person. Watch your gestures.
- Never throw things in anger or disgust.

Notes:

Know How to Manage Your Anger and Emotions

Try to figure out and understand your emotions. Do you know what makes you tick? Do you know what will set you off? Self-awareness is a critical tool. Practice this skill, and use it wisely.

- Know who is angry and why they are angry—including yourself.
- Try not to let things escalate. Smaller issues are easier to solve.
- Explore and seek out solutions to any issue.
- Find someone to help if needed to facilitate problem solving.
- Manage your own stress.
- Life is too short. Do not get angry over stupid things.
- Look for common ground, and if you are wrong, admit it!
- Reflect and work on the situation.
- *If necessary, try to repair any relationship. Mend some fences.*

At the end of the day, if you know you have anger issues, seek some professional help! If not it could cost you your job or bring legal ramifications. Know thyself!

Notes:

Relationships with Students Must Be Professional

Students are to be treated fairly and with respect. Your interactions should be friendly. However, please understand this: the students have all of the friends that they need. They do not need any more friends. I hope you see the difference. You are the authority figure. You can never abuse this relationship. Take time to think about the following:

- Avoid touching students. Keep your hands to yourself.
- Avoid being left alone with students.
- Never leave a class or students in general unsupervised.
- Watch how you say things. Students don't understand sarcasm and ridicule.
- Be proactive in your supervision, especially in the cafeteria, on the playground, and on field trips.
- When you are angry, take a break.
- Never drive students in your private vehicle. Check your specific board policy.
- Document, document, document.
- Avoid unnecessary communications—for example, late night calls, emails, or text messages.
- Do not socialize with students. You are looking for trouble.
- Do not use physical force with students. Learn your school policy and procedure on this topic. If a physical altercation occurs with a student, give a strong verbal command with specific directions. Seek assistance. Prevent others from participating.

Let's take a look at a few examples:

- A student is wearing a hat. You snatch it off. We could have a problem.
- You block the doorway and challenge a student to get by you. We could have a problem.
- You tell a student to sit down and he refuses. You go over and push him down in the seat. We could have a problem.

Any time you touch a student, you are potentially vulnerable to some questions.

It is important to review *hugging*. We could perhaps argue that students need that hug. I do not necessarily agree with you. Okay, I get it. That Kindergarten student is upset, and they need that motherly hug. But why are you hugging a senior in high school? Why a middle school student? I have seen too many bad things happen as a result of a hug. Be careful.

Notes:

You Must Report All Suspected Cases of Child Abuse

You see it. You recognize it. You know it. Now what do you do? You report it! Laws vary by state, but no matter what state you are in, if you suspect child abuse, it is incumbent on the person who suspects it to report it. You must make a *good faith effort* to report all suspected cases of abuse. Just telling someone else or your boss is not enough. You must pick up the phone and call the authorities. You may have a dual reporting system where you must call both the police and a state agency. Do not wait. Have all of the personal information ready when you make the call and the reasons that you suspect abuse. An administrator can help you with the process. Know your district's policy on this topic. A failure to report could result in your criminal prosecution.

Notes:

You Must Keep Your Area and Common Areas Safe and Clean and Equipment Well Stocked

Have some personal pride in your work station. Make sure it is safe and clean. You have a responsibility to conduct yourself in a safe and healthy way. Some reminders:

- Keep your area clean, neat, and safe.
- Put things away when you are done.
- Make sure all of your equipment is in good working order.
- Report any potentially dangerous situations immediately. This is especially important on play areas and athletic fields. For example, the physical educator must first check the outdoor area for a class activity. Likewise, the playground staff must ensure that the playground is safe.
- Walk and drive safely on the property.
- Know your tools, and use the right one for the job.
- Report all accidents at once, and see the nurse. Follow the right procedure for any Workers Compensation case.
- Dress in a safe manner for work.

Likewise, treat common areas like your own. You were not raised in a barnyard, so do not act like it!

- Always remember to keep the school's common areas clean and well stocked. If you use a common refrigerator, remove your things when done. Do not let something rot away in there.

- Clean your table of your garbage and spills. Throw trash away. If common equipment is used, return it the way it was given to you. For example, if you borrowed a stapler, do not return it empty.
- Never walk away from a copier and leave it jammed or void of paper. If you do not know how to fix something, ask for help.

Notes:

Read Everything, and When in Doubt, Ask Someone!

When you are new on a job, you will be given a great deal of things to read and review. Read them. If you ever have a question, ask someone. Know your policy manuals and your contract. When the principal sends out a memorandum, read it! If something is posted, read it. Check your email regularly. It is your job to read and comprehend anything that is given to you. Ignorance is no excuse for failing to comply with something. The excuse of "I didn't know" when it was placed in black and white just won't cut it. Once again, you are the adult. Act like one!

Notes:

Your Personal Effects Must Be Secured

Make sure that your pocketbook, phone, and computer remain locked up when not in use. Things have a way of disappearing when they are left unattended in a matter of minutes. Be wise, and take the extra few seconds to secure your personal belongings. I can recall very vividly when a secretary assigned to the school nurse, in a quiet office in the school, got up from her desk to use the lavatory in the nurse's suite and her pocketbook was stolen—all in a matter of seconds. And I hate to blame the victim, but why didn't she just lock it in her desk? She was too trusting and just got careless.

Also, never lend your keys out to a student. You never know what they could do with them. You are responsible for your keys. I can vividly recall one time when a person carelessly lost his keys. It forced the district to rekey all of the outside doors to the building—a costly endeavor. And by the way, that person was me! I was lucky that I had enough goodwill built within the district that it was not a fatal mistake for me. You have been warned.

Notes:

Never Be Negligent

Negligence extends well beyond something you may have done. It also addresses things that you did not do but that you were expected to do. A brief common definition of negligence is *the failure to take proper care when doing something* (Google).

Let's make sure you keep the following points in mind:

- Never leave students unattended and unsupervised, even for a minute.
- Never use any form of corporal punishment. Keep your hands to yourself.
- Do not send a disruptive student to the office unattended. Follow your specific school procedures here.
- Never give any form of medicine to a student. This includes something as simple as a cough drop or aspirin. I had a custodian one time who was very well-liked by the students. He was asked by a student for an aspirin. He happily gave it to her. We escaped a potentially major problem.
- Report all accidents at once.
- Know all emergency drill procedures.
- Always be able to account for your students. If you cannot, contact the administration at once.
- If a student is ill, seek assistance at once.
- Never let students leave the premises.
- Avoid introducing controversial topics in your classroom without the approval of the administration.
- Never be left alone with a student. Make sure all offices have windows. Do not use secluded closets as a teaching station. This may happen frequently in the area of music and art. Being alone

in a closet with a student is looking for trouble. I know this is true because I had to deal with a very bad situation where a teacher abused students in an anteroom to a stage. You have been warned.

- Protect students from all equipment.
- Make sure all videos are approved by the administration.
- Know your school's policy on student teacher interns.
- Be especially aware and tuned into any suicidal threats and ideations. It seems as though we are having to deal with this at a very early age now. *Follow your district policy on this.* Never leave this student unattended, even to send him or her to the office. Report this at once. Do not wait until the end of the day. I recall a situation where at around four p.m. a teacher casually walked into my office and told me that she had read some troubling suicide threats in a student's journal. Now she was worried. This happened at ten a.m. Whys did she wait? Who knows? I am happy to say that we averted a tragedy here, but it could have been catastrophic.

Why do these types of issues always happen late in the day? Why do they always seem to happen on a Friday or the day before a vacation? Be extra vigilant on these days.

Notes:

Substitutes Are Expected to Teach

Some general substitute teacher guidelines; always follow your district's specific guidelines

- Have the right attitude and energy for the job. Be a positive influence.
- Be patient.
- Listen to others.
- Be consistent, clear, and fair.
- Proactively supervise the students.
- Do not get upset if an administrator visits your classroom. Good administrators are visible and in classes.
- Follow the teacher's lesson plans—*teach*. Have a back-up plan. If you are good, the students will quickly learn your style and are more apt to be respectful and comply.
- Arrive early and familiarize yourself with the building and standard procedures of the school.
- Know the class rules.
- Seek out a neighboring teacher, introduce yourself, and know who to contact if you need help.
- Always take accurate attendance.
- Know accident procedures. Know where the nurse is located. Never move an injured student. Stay calm, look calm, keep everyone safe, and provide lifesaving first aid if needed.
- Never give any medications to a student, even cough drop or aspirin.

- Know if there are any allergies in the room, such as nuts, milk, wheat, beestings, etc. You must be very vigilant in this area. One slip-up could be fatal.
- Establish a good rapport with students. You are not their friend.
- Keep your perspective and patience.
- Avoid all power struggles with students. This is not a win/lose game. Believe me, you will never win this little battle, and you will get wounded in the process.
- Get help when needed.
- Leave a follow-up report with the classroom teacher.
- Pay attention. You are not there to read the newspaper.
- Never resort to any mass punishments with students.
- Do not embarrass students. Do not yell and scream, and do not use sarcasm.
- Treat all students with respect.
- If a physical altercation develops, give a strong verbal command to stop, and follow specific school guidelines.
- Collect all assignments from students.
- Return any keys or handouts to the office.
- Know how to use teacher editions.
- Follow classroom procedures for daily activities of the building, such as lunch money collection.
- Make sure you know the district's mental health policies, especially suicide plans. Always report your thoughts at once. Do not wait until the end of the day, and always keep your eyes on a student of concern.

Notes:

Bring on the Students

Game planning is over. It is kick-off time. You toiled long and hard to land this position. You have practiced and prepared. Now it is time to execute. Let me share several last-minute reminders that you must never forget.

- Schools are about students, not adults.
- This is a people industry. It is always about the relationships that you establish.
- It is all about effort and attitude. Choose that positive attitude every day!
- Stay positive and strong. Avoid being drawn to the "dark side." You are the "force."
- Learn from your mistakes.

Congratulations. No matter what your role and job title may be, you have chosen a very noble profession. *Respect it! You must be a champion! You must be a winner! Good luck!*

Notes:

Acronyms and Abbreviations

The world of education is filled with hundreds of acronyms and abbreviations. There truly is an educational jargon. Below is a sampling of popular acronyms and abbreviations that you might find helpful. There are many books published with a more complete list. These are not state specific inasmuch as your state may have an additional unique set of acronyms.

ADA	Americans with Disabilities Act or Average Daily Attendance
ADHD	Attention Deficit Hyperactivity Disorder
AP	Advanced Placement
ASL	American Sign Language
AT	Assistive Technology
AU	Autistic/Autism
AUP	Acceptable Use Policy
AYP	Annual Yearly Progress
BOE	Board of Education
CB	College Board
CDC	Center for Disease Control
CE	Character Education
CST	Child Study Team
DI	Direct Instruction
DOE	Department of Education
DOH	Department of Health
EAP	Employee Assistance Program
ECERS	Early Childhood Environment Rating Scale

ED	Emotionally Disturbed
ELL	English Language Learner
ERIC	Education Resource Information Center
ESL	English as a Second Language
ESSA	Elementary and Secondary Education Act
ESY	Extended School Year
ETS	Educational Testing Services
FAPE	Free and Appropriate Public Education
FBA	Functional Behavioral Analysis
FERPA	Family Education Rights and Privacy Act
GATE	Gifted and Talented Education
GE	General Education
GPA	Grade Point Average
HI	Hearing Impaired or Home Instruction
HHS	US Department of Health and Human Services
HMO	Health Maintenance Organization
HOTS	Higher Order Thinking Skills
HQT	Highly Qualified Teacher
IDEA	Individuals with Disability Education Act
IEP	Individual Education Program
ISS/SS	In-School Suspension/Out of School Suspension
IQ	Intelligence Quotient
K-12, PK-12	Kindergarten through grade twelve, pre-kindergarten through grade twelve
KWL	Know, Want to Learn, Learned
LD	Learning Disabled
LEA	Local Education Authority
LRE	Least Restrictive Environment
MH	Multiply Handicapped
MOU	Memorandum of Understanding
NAESP	National Association of Elementary School Principals
NASSP	National Association of Secondary School Principals
NBCT	National Board Teacher Certified

NEA	National Education Association
NIH	National Institute of Health
NHS	National Honor Society
OCD	Obsessive Compulsive Disorder
OCR	Office for Civil Rights
OSHA	Occupational Safety and Health Association
OT	Occupational Therapy
PAARC	Partnership for Assessment of Readiness for College and Careers
PE	Physical Education
PL	Public Law
PSAT	At one time it stood for the Preliminary Scholastic Aptitude Test. It is also the National Merit Scholarship Qualifying Test. Now it is considered just the Preliminary SAT. (see SAT)
PT	Physical Therapy
PTA/PTO	Parent-Teacher Association or Parent-Teacher Organization
PTSD	Post-Traumatic Stress Disorder
RFP	Request for Proposals
RIF	Reduction in Force
RTI	Response to Intervention
SAP	Student Assistance Program
SAT	At one time it stood for Scholastic Aptitude Test and then evolved to the Scholastic Assessment Test and now it has evolved to stand for nothing.
SES	Socioeconomic Status
SGO	Student Growth Objective
SIP	School Improvement Plan
SLD	Specific Learning Disability
SPED	Special Education
SS	Social Security
SSA	Social Security Administration

STEM	Science, Technology, Engineering, and Math
STEAM	Science, Technology, Engineering, Art, and Math
SRO	School Resource Officer
SWBAT	Student Will Be Able To
TE/TM	Teacher's Edition/Teacher's Manual
TBD	To Be Determined
USDOE	United States Department of Education
WISC	Wechsler Intelligence Scale for Children
504 PLAN	An education plan for a child with an identified disability that will provide modifications and accommodation to the child

Who? What? Where?

It is critical that you know who to contact or where to go when you need help to complete a task. Use these pages to answer your questions specific to your district.

- Health benefits:
- Technology issues:
- Paycheck questions:
- Parking lot procedures:
- Security issues:
- Identification badge:
- Signing In /Signing out:
- Reporting an absence:
- Lunch and break procedure:
- Preferred method of communication in the district:
- Evaluators:
- Job description:
- Policy manuals:
- Association Representatives:
- Copy of contract:
- Daily schedule:
- Keys:
- Coffee and food policy:
- Copy Machine Procedures:
- Nurse:
- Laminator procedures:
- Employee Assistance Programs:
- Accident reporting:
- Faculty staff dining:

- Child Abuse Reporting:
- Addressing each other, i.e. Mr. Ms. Firs names:
- Employee mail:
- Purchasing items for school:
- Work orders
- Chain of command/ Table of organization:
- Coworkers:
- Map of school:
- PTA/PTO:

References

Christensen, J. (1998). The Fish Philosophy. Retrieved from http://www.fishphilosophy.com/fish-philosophy-story/#four-practices.

Fulghum,R.L. (1986). *All I Really Needed to Know I Learned in Kindergarten: Uncommon Thoughts on Common Things.* New York: Random House Inc.

Gruenert,S. and Whitaker, T. (2015). *School Culture Rewired: How to Define, Assess and Transform It.* Virginia: Association of Supervision and Curriculum Development.

Hindy, J. (2017). 8 Ways to Receive Feedback and Turn Them Into Your Strengths. Retrieved from https://www.lifehack.org/articles/work/8-ways-to-receive-feedback-and-turn-them-into-your-strengths.html.

McCarthy, D. (2018). 18 Ways to Receive Feedback. Retrieved from https://greatleadereshipbydan,2018/1/18/tips-for-receiving-feedback-html.

About the Author

Edward Yergalonis served for thirty-eight years in public education, most of those years in administration. In addition to being a teacher and a coach, he has served as an assistant principal, principal of a middle school, principal of a high school, an assistant superintendent, and finally retiring as the superintendent of the Rahway Public Schools, in Rahway, New Jersey. He holds degrees from the College of William and Mary and the University of Cincinnati. He has widely presented and is the author of articles mostly focusing on leadership. He has served on the National Urban Task Force for the National Association of Secondary School principals and the College Scholarship Service Assembly for the College Board. He currently serves as a mentor to new principals and writes a weekly blog focusing on educational leadership that can be found at www.expectingexcellence.net.

Acknowledgments

A big thank you is extended to all of the teachers, coaches, secretaries, custodians, paraprofessionals, safety officers, substitutes, and fellow administrators who come to work each and every day doing their best for our children. A special thank you is extended to all of my colleagues I have personally worked with throughout the years.

Mrs. Mary Yergalonis, my wife, for serving as my personal copy editor and biggest supporter.

Mrs. Tiffany Lynch-Beer for preventing me from butchering the English language.

Ms. Felicia Basso, a working school administrative assistant, who has provided valuable insight into this work.